# CATHEDRALS

Text: **Tom Stanier and Harry Sutton**
Illustrations: **Joseph McEwan**
Advisor: Canon Peter Brett

| Contents: | Pages |
| --- | --- |

**BBC Books in association with Heritage Books**

# Houses of God

God is worshipped in many different ways all over the world. We call the different ways 'religions'. A religion is a set of rules for pleasing God and living a good life. Most religions have priests who keep the rules and help people to know God's will by holding services in places of worship. On these two pages you can see some of the fine Houses of God built for religions of many different kinds.

**1** One of the great religious places of the world is at Mecca in Arabia.
The Great Mosque is the sacred place of the Muslim religion, Muslims from all over the world travel to Mecca once in their lifetime. It is part of their duty to God.

**2** At Amritsar, in Northern India, there is a beautiful temple set within a lake. This is the sacred place of the Sikh religion.

**3** Burma is a Buddhist country. This is the Shwe Dagon temple in Rangoon. Its spires and roofs are plated in gold.

**4** Benares, on the banks of the River Ganges, is a most holy place for the Hindu religion. Hindus travel from all over the world to bathe in the river, which is sacred in their faith.

**6** Buddhism is a popular religion in Japan. This is the Golden Hall of the Horyuji Temple. It was built in 670 AD and is the oldest temple in Japan.

**5** There are many beautiful Hindu temples in India. This is the Temple of Arunachaleswara in Tamilmadu State. It is a favourite place of pilgrimage.

**7** Wherever Christians live, they build churches for the worship of God. This is the Christian Cathedral at Lusaka in Zambia. It was opened in 1962 by the Queen Mother.

**8** This is All Saints Cathedral at Aklavik in Canada. It is called 'The Cathedral of the Arctic'. Consecrated in 1939, it was built of timber from British Colombia and can hold 280 people.

# The first cathedrals

The story of our cathedrals starts nearly two thousand years ago, with the death of Jesus Christ. He died on a cross in Jerusalem. The religion He taught in His lifetime, which came to be called Christianity, spread slowly at first. The Romans, under whose laws Christ was crucified, outlawed Christianity and put to death anybody practising it.

**1** Britain under the Romans was prosperous. At first, however, it was a pagan country for the Romans brought their own religion with them. They worshipped many different gods.

**2** Then, in the year AD 312, the Roman emperor Constantine the Great became a Christian and the new religion quickly spread through the Roman Empire. Constantine himself visited Britain and his father died in the Roman city of York.

**3** The Romans built many churches in Britain. This drawing shows how a Roman church in Britain may have looked.

**4** The Romans ruled Britain for nearly four hundred years. But then, everything began to change. Tribes from the east attacked Rome and the Roman legions in Britain were sent home to defend their own country. With no armies to oppose them, Picts and Scots from the north and Saxons from across the North Sea invaded Britain.

**5** The Saxons were farming people who had no use for the fine towns built by the Romans. They were not Christians and the Roman churches were allowed to fall into ruin.

**6** Then, in the year 596 AD, Pope Gregory the Great decided that Christianity should be brought back to Britain. From Rome he sent a teacher named Augustine to convert the Saxons. With forty companions, Augustine arrived in Kent and his first work was to repair a ruined church in the town of Canterbury.

**7** During the next two centuries, Britain became a Christian country and many hundreds of churches were built. Most of them were small and made of wood with thatched roofs. This is a picture of the Saxon church of St Andrew at Greenstead in Essex. Its walls are built of split oak logs and it originally had a wooden tower.

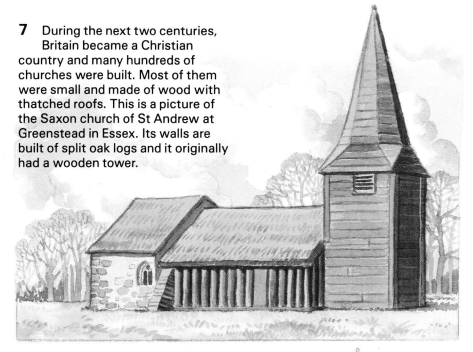

**8** Britain was not allowed to remain at peace for very long. In the year 793, the famous monastery of Lindisfarne was attacked and destroyed by a powerful fleet from Denmark. It was the start of the Viking invasions.

**9** The Vikings were pagans and, once more, Christianity in Britain was under attack. Churches and monasteries were robbed and burned; their monks and priests were killed.

**10** King Alfred the Great, who was a devout Christian, fought against the invaders and after years of struggle, he defeated them. Guthrum, king of the Vikings, became a friend of King Alfred and was converted to Christianity.

**11** King Alfred died in the year 899 and for the next hundred years churches and cathedrals were built in great numbers. By the year 1000 there were fifteen Saxon cathedrals and many of the churches were large and stone-built like this one in the picture.

**12** Then, in the year 1066, there came another invasion. The Normans stormed ashore at Hastings. The story of our present cathedrals was about to start.

# The cathedral builders

The Normans soon set about tearing down the cathedrals built by the Saxons. They rebuilt them on a much grander scale. But then the Norman cathedrals were rebuilt in their turn and at each reconstruction a different style was used. On page 27 you can see examples of all these styles. On these two pages you can see how cathedrals were built in the 'Gothic' style.

**1** First, suitable stone had to be found. The master mason, who was the architect appointed by the bishop, would draw plans. Then he would visit a quarry and decide how many blocks of stone he would need to buy. In this picture you can see:

**a** — quarrymen hammering wooden wedges into holes made in the stone bed. When the wedges are soaked with water, they will expand and split the stone along its natural grain. It can then be removed as a block.

**b** — other quarrymen using a crane called a 'windlass' to lift blocks of stone from the quarry.

**c** — men cutting stone to the size needed by the architect.

**d** — a quarryman trimming stone. He is chipping it to shape using a metal tool.

**e** — stone bought by the architect being loaded for the journey to the building site. The crane they are using is called 'sheer legs'.

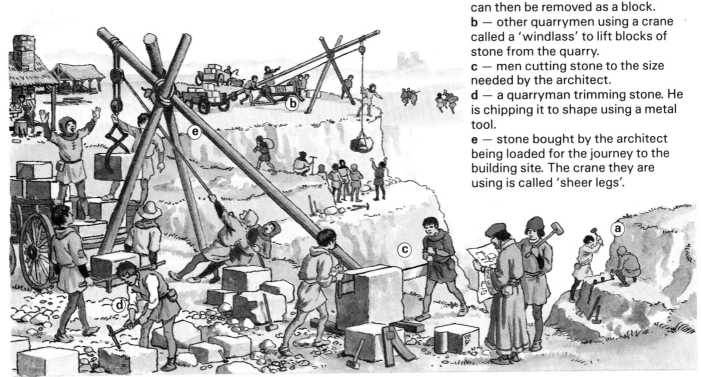

**2** This picture shows the stone from the quarry arriving at the site of the cathedral building.

**a** — trees have been felled and timber cut from them is being stacked ready for use.

**b** — the men building the walls are called 'stone masons'.

**c** — the long, low building is the masons' 'lodge' where they lived during the building of the cathedral. Part of the lodge was also their workshop.

**d** — these are the carpenters who worked with the masons. They built the scaffolding and also wooden supports called 'formers', which held the stone arches together as they were being constructed. When the arch was complete, the former was removed.

**e** — this is the blacksmith who made tools for the masons and carpenters and kept them sharp.

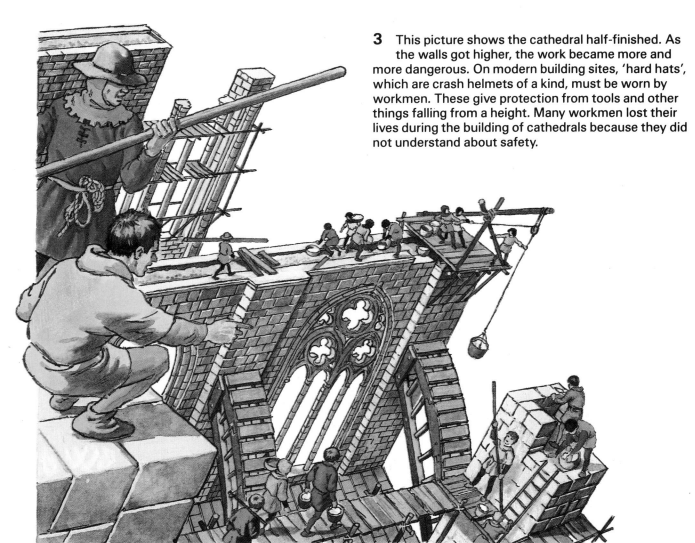

**3** This picture shows the cathedral half-finished. As the walls got higher, the work became more and more dangerous. On modern building sites, 'hard hats', which are crash helmets of a kind, must be worn by workmen. These give protection from tools and other things falling from a height. Many workmen lost their lives during the building of cathedrals because they did not understand about safety.

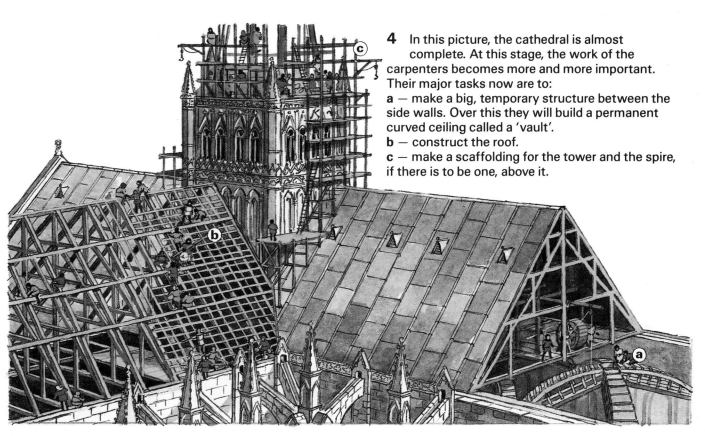

**4** In this picture, the cathedral is almost complete. At this stage, the work of the carpenters becomes more and more important. Their major tasks now are to:

**a** — make a big, temporary structure between the side walls. Over this they will build a permanent curved ceiling called a 'vault'.

**b** — construct the roof.

**c** — make a scaffolding for the tower and the spire, if there is to be one, above it.

# The artists in wood and stone

Working alongside the carpenters and stone masons there were artists whose materials were stone and wood. Except for porches and entrance doors, which were often finely carved, the work of the woodcarvers was inside the cathedral. The sculptors worked in stone which could withstand the weather. Much of their work was outside. In the early days of cathedrals, both wood and stone carvings were painted in bright colours but this came to be thought unsuitable for places of worship and much of it was removed. Original colour can still be seen in some cathedrals and on page 31, advice is given about where to look for colour traces.

a

b

**1** Very early wood carving can easily be recognised in cathedrals because the carpenters who did the carving copied the way sculptors carved stone. As can be seen in **(a)** above, their work was very plain. Later, as in **(b)** above, they learned to produce fine detail, even more elaborate than that achieved in stone.

**2** Through the centuries, carpenters discovered many clever ways of joining lengths of wood together to make roofs, ceilings and spires. Their methods were now used by the woodcarvers. They were able to join sections together to make structures like this row of seats for a cathedral. They are called 'choir stalls' and are places for clergy to sit in the choir — see picture 2 on page 30.

**3** Everywhere in cathedrals you can see the work of the stone-carving mason. The delicate stone framework of the windows; the columns and ceiling decorations; the stone traceries that add beauty to otherwise plain walls. All that is the work of the stone-carver. But it is in the carving of lifelike figures that their best work can be seen. The sculptor began with a block of stone and drawings of the figure he wishes to produce. He visualised the figure as it would fit into the inside of the stone block.

**4** Stone had to be removed from the block in order to carve out the rough shape of the figure. A block like this one could weigh more than a tonne and it was hard work getting rid of the unwanted stone. The sculptor could split away larger sections by means of wedges, as was done by the quarrymen (page 6 picture 1). The rest had to be removed with a heavy hammer and a steel tool called a 'pitcher'.

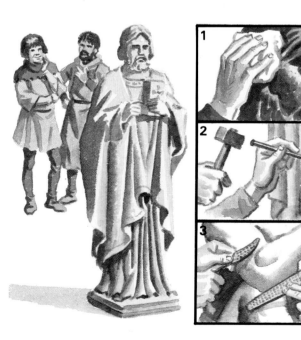

**5** The sculptor then started to carve the stone into the shape of the drawing. Other tools, which removed less stone, were now used. The sculptor could see the figure 'emerging' from the block.

**6** When the figure was completely carved from the block, the stone had to be finished off with other tools to give it a smooth surface. If the stone was hard granite, **(1)** the sculptor used carborundum powder which gave it a high polish. **(2)** Fine chisels were used to give a smooth finish to sandstone or limestone. **(3)** Marble was smoothed with metal tools called 'rasps' and 'rifflers'. It was then polished with a special powder.

# Stained glass windows

In the days before gas and electricity, people had to rely far more upon natural daylight for work and play. They had only oil lamps and candles which gave poor light and were expensive. Most people went to bed when it was dark and started work at dawn. To let daylight into their cathedrals, the stone masons, with wonderful skill, built huge windows into the walls. They not only let in sunshine but also made delicate patterns all round the interior. These beautiful windows gave another artist, the glass painter, an opportunity to add his skill to the building of the cathedral. The glaziers filled the windows with pictures in brilliant colours.

**1**   The shape of the window was first drawn to the correct size and the stones were cut.

**2**   This is a picture of the east window in Gloucester cathedral as it would have looked before glass was fitted.

**3**   This is how the same window looks now, complete with its stained glass.

**4**   Glass was made by mixing sand, lime and potash from wood ash, and melting them together in clay pots in a furnace.

**6**   To make sheets of glass, the end of a metal blowpipe was dipped into molten glass and a lump collected on the end of it. Then, by blowing down the pipe, a glass bubble was formed at the end.

**8**   The ends were then cut off to make a cylinder of glass. A red hot iron was used to cut along one side of the cylinder.

**5**   The furnace was shaped like a beehive. The fire was lit at the bottom and the pots were heated in the compartment above. The pots had to be made white-hot and to get them as hot as that, boys were kept very busy, stoking the furnace with logs.

**7**   By swinging the bubble, the glass blower could make it stretch under its own weight into a long bottle-shape.

**9**   The cut cylinder was then put into the furnace to be softened so that it could be opened up into a flat sheet.

**10** By mixing other chemicals with the sand, lime and potash, glass of different colours could be made. White glass could be coated with colour by dipping the glass bubble into a crucible of molten coloured-glass. Other glass could be coloured throughout.

**11** To make a window of stained glass, the design was first drawn, either on a white-washed table or on parchment. The heavy black lines showed where the lead-jointing would be.

**12** To cut the glass roughly to shape, the glass-worker touched it with a hot iron and then poured cold water on to the heated spots. This caused the glass to crack and break along the line of hot spots.

**13** To cut small sections to fit into the picture, workmen 'nibbled' at the glass edges with a tool called a 'grozing iron'.

**14** The glass pieces could then be fitted together on the pattern and painting could begin. The paint used was a special kind which would melt and become part of the glass when it was heated.

**15** When a section of glass was ready, it was placed in a metal tray and the paint was 'fired' — that is, melted into the glass. The furnace was not hot enough to melt the glass itself.

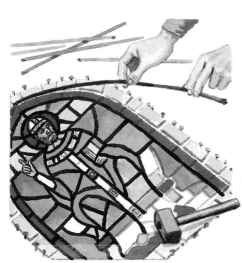

**16** The glass was now ready to be fitted together. A strong band of lead was fixed round the outside to make the section strong.

**17** Lengths of grooved lead, called 'cames', were fitted between each section of glass. The joints were made with drops of molten solder (lead mixed with tin).

**18** Finally the section of window was put into place. It would have to stand up to the wind and rain outside and, to make it strong enough, metal bars were fixed into the stone surrounds to hold the glass securely in place.

# Marvels of cathedrals

The Normans were in a hurry to build huge castles and cathedrals to impress the people of Britain whom they had conquered. They brought with them from Normandy ways of building which were new to Britain, but as we have seen, their methods soon gave way to a style we call 'Gothic'.

Our present cathedrals are the result of many changes through the centuries. Old and new, they all contain marvels — of artistry and craftsmanship, and of grandeur. Their builders did their best work for the glory of God.

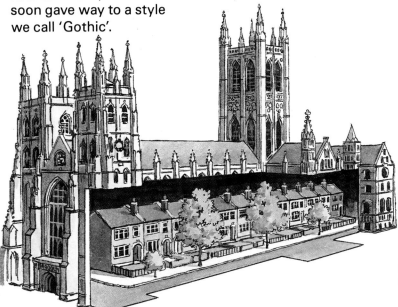

**1** Most cathedrals are long and tall, but it is not easy to appreciate just how big they are. This is a drawing of Canterbury cathedral. There is room inside for a street of houses — and for tall trees as well.

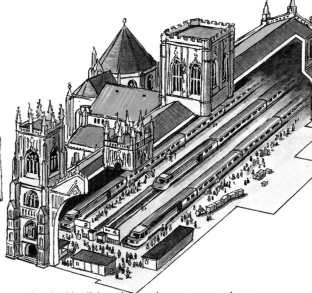

**2** The cathedral builders knew how to span huge areas with arches and columns. This is a picture of York minster, which is 148 metres long and 31 metres wide across the nave. That is big enough for a complete railway station to fit inside.

**3** The stone spire of Salisbury cathedral was built more than 600 years ago, yet it is 124 metres tall — the height of a 30-storey tower block.

**4** The Great Fire of London broke out because most of the houses in the city were then built of wood with thatched roofs. But the new St Paul's cathedral built to replace the one burned down was built of stone. It's centre dome is so big that there is room at the crossing for a full-size tennis court — and an audience to watch the game.

**5** Most of our cathedrals have stood through all the great events of our history. Standing in front of a cathedral, looking up at it, you are seeing it just as your ancestors may have seen it, many centuries ago.

**6** Many cathedrals began as small churches but have been rebuilt several times to provide for a growing population. In some of them the remains of older churches can still be seen and many are very old indeed. This picture is of the crypt, (underground chapel), of Ripon cathedral. It is all that is left of a church built more than a thousand years ago.

**7** Cathedrals were built on a very grand scale so that large numbers of people could worship at the same time. There is far more room in them than in any big, modern theatre or cinema. There were 2650 guests at the wedding of the Prince and Princess of Wales. But the total number of people in St. Paul's cathedral that day exceeded 4000 including clergy, two choirs, an orchestra and television crews.

**8** Stone masons were able to practise their skills in cathedrals, especially at the entrances which were always made as impressive as possible. Statues and stone decorations were used to give a rich effect, like these which can be seen on the west front of Wells cathedral. Many modern sculptors and masons are at work, repairing damage from the weather and by air pollution.

# Monks in cathedrals

Most cathedrals were served by monks in Saxon times and the Normans established monasteries beside many of their newly founded cathedrals. At these cathedrals, the bishop was abbot (head) of the monastery and the monks served the cathedral. On these two pages you can see the layout of a typical monastic cathedral.

**1 Bishop's lodgings.** The bishop and his staff had their own residence at the cathedral. It was usually a large building with a dining hall, chapel, living quarters and rooms for guests.

**2 Chapter house.** The chapter house was a meeting place where the affairs of the cathedral could be discussed. There was a special place for the bishop at meetings but he usually left matters in the care of the Prior. He was head of the cathedral monastery under the bishop. It was called a 'chapter' house because a chapter of the Rule of St Benedict was read aloud before every meeting.

**3 The dormitory.** This is where the monks slept, and in the early days, the beds were in two rows as in a hospital ward. Later, however, partitions were put up in most dormitories to give the monks more privacy. Below the dormitory there was often a 'warming room' where the monks could gather in front of a nice log fire after early morning service in winter.

**4 The cloister.** This was a covered way used by the monks for many purposes. The centre of the cloister was an open area where herbs and vegetables could be grown. The cloister arches overlooking the central area were often fitted with glass or shutters. The monks had desks along the south cloister where the light was best for writing and studying.

**5 The monastery farm.** Unless the cathedral was right in the middle of a town, there was usually land nearby which belonged to the cathedral and could be farmed. The usual farm buildings were needed: stables for the farm horses, grain stores, pig styes, etc.

**6 The infirmary.** This was the hospital for monks who were ill or too old and infirm to live the hard daily life of the monastery. The food was better in the infirmary and there was more comfort.

Granary

Prior Hall

**7 The refectory.** This was the monks' dining hall. The prior and the senior monks sat at the high table. The rest of the monks sat at long tables which ran the length of the refectory. High up in the south wall there was a pulpit from where one of the monks read from the Bible during meals — which had to be eaten in silence. The bishop had a separate dining hall of his own.

**8 Lay brothers and townsfolk.** To help them, the monks had a large staff. There were skilled workers — carpenters, blacksmiths, cooks, bakers and gardeners — who took some religious vows and were called 'lay brothers'. Labouring work was done by local people on a daily basis.

Bakery

Almoner's House

Cellarer's

# Secular cathedrals

The monks gave up ordinary life and shut themselves up in monasteries to devote all their time to prayer and study. There were others, however, who felt that they could best serve God by living amongst ordinary people and helping them to become good Christians. They also took religious vows but were allowed to own property and to live a normal life. These were called 'secular' clergy. King Henry the Eighth closed all the monasteries (see page 24) and since then, all our cathedrals have been served by secular clergy. The pictures on these two pages show the people responsible for the day-to-day work of a secular cathedral at the time of Henry the Eighth.

**1** This is the bishop. He was a busy person with many responsibilities outside his cathedral church. The area of country in his care was called his 'diocese'. This might cover several counties with hundreds of villages, many towns and the cathedral city itself. Churches had to be visited regularly and there were priests to appoint and advise. The early bishops, like the one in the picture, were often rich and powerful, with large estates, castles and palaces. Some lived almost like kings. They were indeed, advisers to kings and queens and some rarely, if ever, visited their own cathedrals.

**3** One of the most important of the canons was the Precentor or Cantor. He was in charge of the cathedral choir, setting the pitch of the singing and teaching the choirboys to sing together and in tune. He was also responsible for the music chosen for each service. Music and song has always been important in cathedrals and the precentor had to have great musical knowledge. He appointed and trained the musicians and supplied the instruments.

**2** Because the bishop had to be free for other work, another senior clergyman had to look after the day-to-day running of the cathedral. This was the Dean. To help him he had a group of clergy called 'canons', who formed a 'committee' called the cathedral 'chapter'. The dean and chapter met in the chapter house, often a very beautiful building like the one in this picture, for their discussions.

**4** The next most important canon was the Chancellor. At this time, all learning was centred on the church, for the monks and clergy were almost the only people able to read and write. The chancellor was responsible for schools run by the cathedrals which were for the sons of merchants and others who wanted to be trained for the church. The chancellor was also keeper of the great seal of the cathedral. Without this, no document dealing with cathedral business was legal.

**5** The busiest canon was the Treasurer. He had care of the treasures of gold and silver which belonged to the cathedral and also of all the things needed for the daily services. He provided the wine, incense, charcoal and candles used in the Mass. He was also in charge of bell-ringing. The repair of the fabric of the cathedral was one of his important duties.

**6** The dean and the canons lived in fine houses near the cathedral. Many of these houses can still be seen in the 'cathedral close' of our cathedrals today. With so many duties, the canons needed assistants to help them and they each employed priests called 'vicars', or 'minor canons'. These assistants also lived near the cathedral in their own close. This picture is of the vicars' close at Chichester cathedral. It was built in the 14th century.

**7** All the priests in cathedrals said Mass every day as a personal act of worship. Many altars were needed and these were set up in chapels and along the walls. Each altar was dedicated to a saint. Today, all the cathedral priests celebrate Mass together.

**8** The complete foundation of a secular cathedral in about the year 1500 was very large. Here you can see them assembled outside their cathedral:
**a** — the bishop and his chaplains
**b** — the dean and sub-dean (his assistant)
**c** — the precentor with his chorister and musicians
**d** — the chancellor with his school masters and pupils
**e** — the treasurer with his bell-ringers, carpenters, masons, glaziers, laundry-maids, cooks, bakers, nightwatchmen and gardeners,

**f** — the vicars or minor canons,
**g** — the chantry priests and their assistant priests or acolytes.

# A cathedral 500 years ago

William the Conquerer and the Norman kings who followed him, were strong supporters of the church. Under them, the wealth and power of the clergy grew and by 1509, when Henry the Eighth came to the throne, they were at the height of their power. The cathedrals, with their splendid treasures and processions of richly-robed priests, were places of wonder to the common people. The pictures on these two pages show some of the more important events that took place in cathedrals at that time.

**1** On Sundays and feast days, the bishop, or the dean, went in procession round the cathedral. They moved from altar to altar, blessing each one as they went.

The leader of the procession was the **'virger' (1)**, and he carried the virge which was originally a rod used to beat people out of the path of the procession. Next came the **aquabajulus (2)**, who carried a bowl of holy water and a sprinkler with which to sprinkle water on each altar as it was blessed. The **cross** came next, carried by the **crucifer (3)** and he was followed by two **acolytes (4)** holding lighted candles. Next in the procession was the **thurifer (5)** who swung a container which gave off scented smoke. This was incense which perfumed the air. The next three priests were the **sub-deacon (6)**, the **deacon (7)**, and the **priest (8)** who celebrated mass when the procession reached the high altar. Next came the **choir boys (9)**, with their choir master and then two lines of **clergy (10)**. Finally came the **bishop (11)** with his two chaplains. The procession wound its way through the cathedral, sometimes going outside to circle the cloister and finally moving right up the centre of the cathedral from the west door where the congregation stood to watch them pass. It was a fine free show of pomp and ceremony and was enjoyed by everybody.

**3** It was generally believed that when specially holy people died and became saints, their dead bodies had miraculous powers. Some were able to heal the sick and others to help people enter heaven when they died. All cathedrals had shrines which held the remains of saints, and people made pilgrimages to them from distant places. They made gifts of money or jewels to gain the saint's favour and enjoyed the journey and visit just as we take holidays. The shrine of St. Thomas (Becket) at Canterbury was the most famous place of pilgrimage.

**2** Some cathedrals had, from ancient times, possessed the right of 'sanctuary'. This meant that nobody could be arrested within the sacred cathedral walls. At Durham cathedral there is still a heavy bronze knocker to be seen on the north door. Those who used it to knock on the door would be given sanctuary at any time of day or night. If they were taken in, the fugitives could confess to their crimes and swear an oath to leave the country, never to return. If they did this, they were taken by the sheriff and passed from constable to constable to be delivered on board a ship at the nearest port.

**5** In every cathedral and at most old churches, there are tombs with inscriptions that name the persons buried below. It was a great honour to be buried inside a cathedral and few people other than royalty and bishops ever found a resting place in one. This drawing shows how burials took place.
**a** — a vault is made below the floor and the coffin is carried into the cathedral in solemn procession.
**b** — a service is held and then the coffin is lowered in to the vault and sealed in.
**c** — in due course, an elaborate monument is built over it.

**4** There could also be fun in cathedrals and one occasion for this was the festival of the 'boy-bishop'. On St Nicholas's Day (6th December each year) one of the choir boys was elected by his fellow choristers to play the part of bishop until Childermas Day, 28th December. With a dean and chapter also chosen from amongst the choir boys, the boy-bishop sat in the real bishop's throne and the boy-canons sat in the canons' stalls for services in the quire. They went in procession outside the cathedral and sightseers enjoyed the scene as a splendid joke. Boy-bishops were elected at Lincoln, Salisbury, Old St Pauls in London, and at York Minster. The festival was ended by order of Henry the Eighth.

# The Pilgrims

There were many pilgrimage shrines in Europe — in England at Canterbury, Santiago in Spain, Cologne in Germany and Rome in Italy. The most famous shrine of all was in Jerusalem, the city where Christ lived and died. On these two pages you can see how Christians made pilgrimages and how they often met difficulties.

1 Going on a pilgrimage was a dangerous business. Many people made a will before they set out. They all wore a special uniform so that they would be recognised as pilgrims on the way.

2 There were guidebooks to tell them where to stay on the journey. The guidebooks contained useful phrases in the local language so that they could make themselves understood and there were also warnings against dangers they might meet.

3 One of the biggest risks was of being attacked by bandits. Many pilgrims were robbed or killed.

4 The inns where they stayed were not very comfortable. Usually pilgrims shared beds and there were plenty of fleas to keep them company as well!

5 Travel by ship was uncomfortable. Food was poor and the ships were overcrowded. To get exercise, pilgrims used to run up and down the rigging, jump up and down on the spot or do weight-lifting. To pass the time, they sang hymns and played games of dice or chess.

**6** The journey was expensive. Apart from the hire of horses and donkeys, officials often had to be bribed for permission to travel.

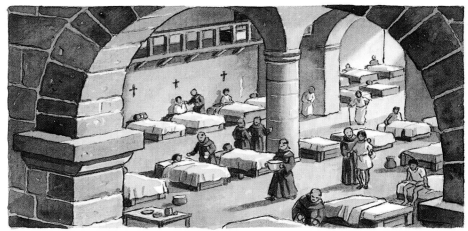

**7** Many pilgrims fell ill and hospitals were set up to care for them. The Hospital of St John of Jerusalem had beds for more than 2000 people. The organisation that ran this hospital still exists today. The St John Ambulance Brigade gives first aid to people at many public events.

**8** There were usually big crowds at the holy places. As well as pilgrims, there were jugglers, conjurers, souvenir-sellers and pickpockets.

**9** Pilgrimages are still made today. Many Catholic Christians go to a famous shrine at Lourdes, in France. They hope that by doing so they will be cured of illnesses.

**10** The world's biggest pilgrimage is still to Mecca where thousands of Muslims gather every year. The journey there, however, is no longer so hard and dangerous. Pilgrims can travel by air these days, but they still wear plain white robes to show that their journey is a religious one.

# Pilgrims' Progress

You will need a dice and some counters for this game. The object is to make a pilgrimage to Canterbury. The winner will be the one first to see the famous Golden Angel shining on the cathedral spire.

**45**

**46** Killed by outlaws — out of game

**47**

**48**

**49** Fine, sunny weather — have another turn

**50**

**44**

**43**

**42**

**41** Muddy road is impassable — miss a turn

**40**

**39**

**38**

**37** Robbed by bandits — miss a turn

**15** Attacked by wolves — miss a turn to recover

**16**

**17**

**18** Catch a fever — miss two turns while in hospital

**19**

**20**

**14**

**13**

**12**

**11** Helpful innkeeper — have another turn

**10**

**9**

**8**

**7** Lose guide book — go back to start

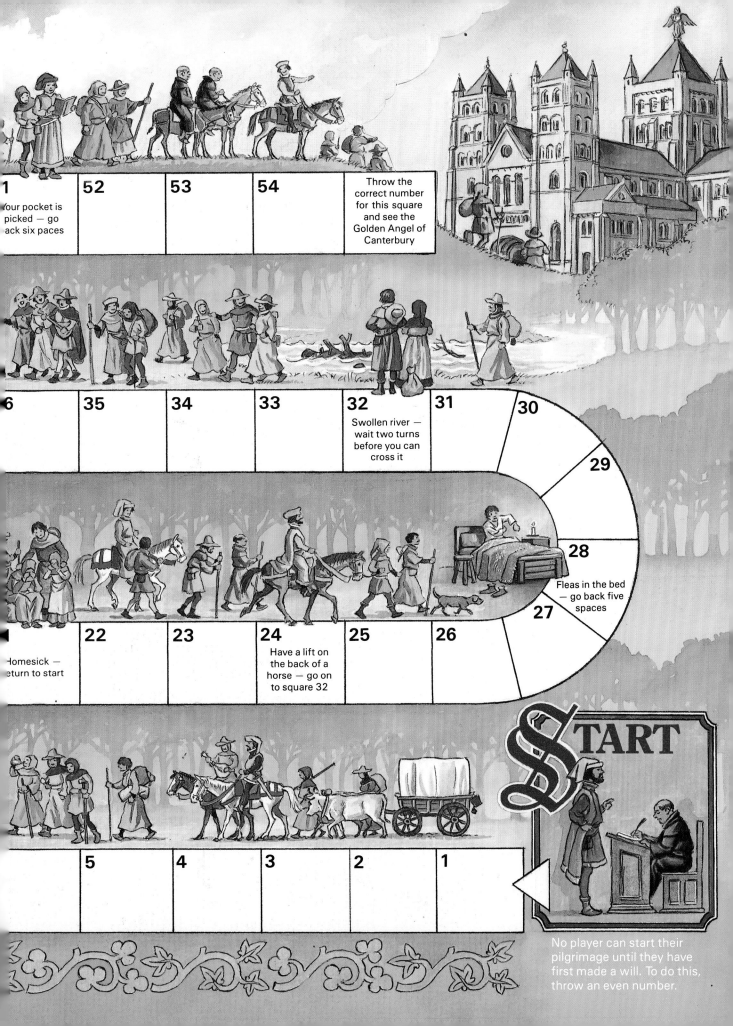

**1**
Your pocket is picked — go back six paces

**52**

**53**

**54**

Throw the correct number for this square and see the Golden Angel of Canterbury

**36**

**35**

**34**

**33**

**32**
Swollen river — wait two turns before you can cross it

**31**

**30**

**29**

**28**
Fleas in the bed — go back five spaces

**27**

**21**
Homesick — return to start

**22**

**23**

**24**
Have a lift on the back of a horse — go on to square 32

**25**

**26**

**START**

**5**

**4**

**3**

**2**

**1**

No player can start their pilgrimage until they have first made a will. To do this, throw an even number.

# Destruction in cathedrals

Although our cathedrals are the most beautiful of all our buildings, they were once even more splendid than we see them now. Twice in our history they have been robbed of their treasures and many of the losses have never been recovered. On these two pages you can see how the loving work of thousands of masons, carpenters, sculptors, artists, silversmiths and many other craftsmen was destroyed.

**1** Until Henry the Eighth quarrelled with him, the Pope in Rome was the supreme head of the church in England, above the king. Henry changed that. He declared himself to be head of the church and refused to accept any interference from Rome.

**2** There were large numbers of monasteries in England at this time. They were wealthy and owned great estates. Many of the abbots and nuns had forgotten their religious duties and were living in luxury. Henry ordered all the monasteries to be closed down. All their wealth was to be taken and put into the royal treasury.

**3** Henry then dealt with the cathedrals which had monks serving them. The monks were turned out and at many cathedrals, their living quarters were knocked down. Their cathedrals were given over to clergy who would obey the king. Some monks did accept the change and became canons and officials, as secular clergy.

**4** The king believed it was wrong for rich people to be able to buy themselves chantries to ensure the safety of their souls after death — when poor people just had to hope for the best! He gave orders for most of the chantries to be knocked down. The money paid for their upkeep was taken into his treasury.

**5** One of the greatest sources of wealth for the cathedrals had been the offerings made by pilgrims. It was well known that some of the shrines contained relics which were not really those of saints at all. Henry had all this swept away and the treasures they had collected were confiscated. The famous shrine of St Thomas was piled high with gold and precious stones. When it was destroyed, the treasures filled two great chests, so heavy that sixteen men were needed to carry it all away. Twenty six carts took the rest of the plunder from Canterbury to London.

**6** Almost exactly one hundred years after the monasteries were closed down, civil war broke out in England. The forces of Parliament declared war on the king. The Roundheads, who fought for parliament under Oliver Cromwell, thought differently about religious matters from most of the bishops and leading men of the Church of England.

**7** The Roundheads particularly disliked the elaborate religious ceremonies of the church. They believed that Christianity should be lived as simply as possible.

**8** The civil war lasted for more than ten years and the cathedrals suffered badly. The Roundheads used some cathedrals as barracks for their soldiers during the war.

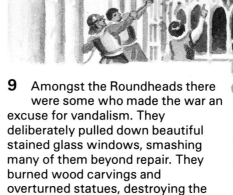

**9** Amongst the Roundheads there were some who made the war an excuse for vandalism. They deliberately pulled down beautiful stained glass windows, smashing many of them beyond repair. They burned wood carvings and overturned statues, destroying the work of centuries.

**10** At Lichfield cathedral a cannon was used to destroy the building and the spire of the central tower collapsed. Lead was taken from the roof to make shot for the Roundhead's muskets. The cathedral was almost completely destroyed and had to be rebuilt after the war.

**11** When the civil war ended the cathedrals and many churches were in a very bad state. It took years to repair them. It was not possible to replace all the fine woodcarving and ancient stained glass but since those days, modern artists and craftsmen have added much that is even more beautiful. Visiting a cathedral today however, it is still possible to see traces of the destruction started by King Henry and completed by Cromwell's soldiers. There are empty alcoves from which statues were torn and plain stonework where there was once bright colour. They are visible evidence of very violent times in our long history.

# History in Cathedrals

Cathedrals and churches are the oldest buildings in Britain. This is because they were built of stone to last forever. Every national event in our long history has left its mark in them, and on these two pages you can see some examples of the evidence to be found.

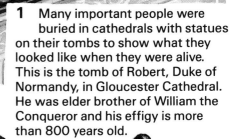

**1** Many important people were buried in cathedrals with statues on their tombs to show what they looked like when they were alive. This is the tomb of Robert, Duke of Normandy, in Gloucester Cathedral. He was elder brother of William the Conqueror and his effigy is more than 800 years old.

**2** There are many fine sculptures in cathedrals which provide us with likenesses of people who lived many years ago. This is the bust of Henry the Fourth who died in 1413. He was the only king buried in Canterbury cathedral.

**3** Ancient machinery can often be seen in cathedrals. In some of them, original cranes used when they were built are still there. This picture is of the oldest clock in England which can be seen in Salisbury cathedral. It was made in 1386 and still works.

**4** This is the Beauchamp tomb in Worcester cathedral. Sir John Beauchamp was steward to King Richard II and was executed for treason. The monks of Worcester thought he was innocent and had his body brought to the cathedral for burial.

**5** In Westminster Abbey, a part has been set aside for the tombs of famous writers. It is called 'Poets' Corner'. It is a place of 'literary history'.

**6** Lines of ancient flags can often be seen high up in some cathedrals. These are usually the flags of local army regiments which were carried in battle and placed in the cathedral in a place of honour at the end of wars.

**7** Sometimes you find very unusual things in cathedrals. This huge carriage was specially built to carry the coffin at the great Duke of Wellington's funeral. It is in the crypt of St Paul's Cathedral in London.

**8** Many great national events are especially marked in cathedrals and churches. This is the Battle of Britain window in Westminster Abbey. It recalls the young men who fought and died during the Second World War to defend Britain in the air.

**9** The fabric of the cathedrals themselves contain history in every wall and arch. As the centuries passed, methods and styles changed and it is possible to tell the age of the different parts of cathedrals from the way they were built. These are the main styles with their dates.

| Saxon | Norman | Early English | Decorated | Perpendicular |
|---|---|---|---|---|
|  |  |  | 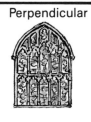 | |
|  |  |  |  | |
| pre-1066 | 1066-1180 | 1160-1310 | 1300-1380 | 1350-1550 |

# Cathedrals now

Through the centuries, the cathedrals of Britain have kept pace with history. They have taken all the great events in their stride. The Normans destroyed cathedrals built by the Saxons — but even greater cathedrals rose in their place. In Tudor times, the church was robbed of its treasures and the monasteries were closed down — but the cathedrals adapted to the changes and went on with their duties to God. Civil war brought pillage and destruction, but the damage was repaired and many of the cathedrals emerged even more splendid than before.

Since then, cities have grown up round most cathedrals, but the towering spires and roofs still rise high above the traffic and busy streets. On these two pages you can see some of the ways in which our cathedrals serve God today.

**2**   There are still craftsmen busy at our ancient cathedrals, repairing and restoring the work of the past.

**1**   Modern artists and craftsmen work to produce beautiful decoration in cathedrals. This picture shows the high altar of the new Coventry cathedral with the famous tapestry of Christ enthroned.

**3**   Cathedrals are places of prayer for the people who live nearby. Services are held daily and on Sundays.

**4**   There are still great occasions in cathedrals. This picture shows the enthronement of an archbishop in progress. It is in York Minster.

**5** Many great state occasions are celebrated in cathedrals. This picture is of the wedding of Prince Charles and Princess Diana at St Paul's Cathedral.

**6** Music has always been important in church life and orchestras with choirs sometimes give special performances in cathedrals, usually to support a charity.

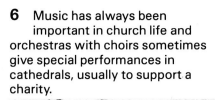

**7** Cathedrals make special arrangements for school visits. Many of them have education centres where children are shown video films and can hear lectures. They are also given work sheets to make their visits more interesting.

**8** Cathedrals are, above all, quiet and tranquil places where people can go just to think and pray.

**9** Many cathedrals have more than a million visitors in a year. They are from every faith and from places all over the world. Even though they may have different religions, people everywhere admire the work of great artists and craftsmen and in our cathedrals they both can be seen at their best. For the skills they have lavished on them have been for the Glory of God.

# Finding your way around cathedrals

When you look round a friend's house, you always know just what rooms to expect and roughly where to find them. Dining room, kitchen, sitting room, bedrooms: you will probably find it rather like your own house for they both have the same purpose — to be a family home.

Cathedrals have a purpose too. To be places where God can be worshipped and where bishops can do their work for God. All cathedrals, therefore, are very much alike in the way they are laid out. The pictures on these two pages may help you to find your way round cathedrals.

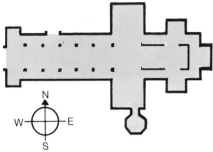

**1** All our cathedrals have their main length lying east and west. This is so that the priest at the high altar can usually pray facing the east which is the direction of the Holy Land where Jesus was born.

**3** The main entrance to a cathedral is always at the western end. The cathedral builders made it as grand as possible so that visitors approaching it for the first time would be impressed by a splendid entrance to God's house.

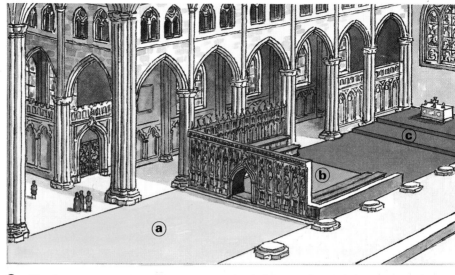

**2** The important parts of cathedrals are also placed at the eastern end. In this picture you can see:
**a** — the public part of the cathedral where people assemble for services. This is called the **nave**.

**b** — this part is called the **choir** and it is here that the clergy have their places and the choir sings.
**c** — this is the most sacred part of the cathedral and is called the **sanctuary.**

**4** All cathedrals were built in the shape of a cross in memory of the crucifixion of Christ. The arms of the cross in a cathedral are called the **transepts.**

**5** Nearly all cathedrals have a tall tower built over the crossing of the transepts. At first, the builders were not quite sure how to make the towers strong enough and many of them fell down. If you stand right under a cathedral tower in the centre of the crossing and then look up, you will see how difficult and dangerous it must have been to build.

**6** The nave of a cathedral is usually separated from the choir by a screening wall called a **pulpitum.** Most were made of stone and had a staircase inside which led to a gallery from which a priest could read the Gospel. In many cathedrals organs have been fitted on top of pulpitums.

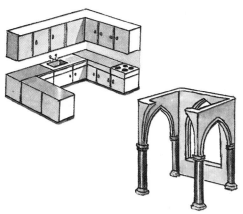

**7** When people want to improve their kitchens, they often buy 'units' which fit together to make a 'fitted kitchen'. The cathedral builders also had a 'unit' to help them. It was made up of four uprights with an arch between each one. These made a rectangular bay. By adding more bays and extending the nave between them, a cathedral could be enlarged, section by section, to make room for more people. Many of our cathedrals were made bigger in this way.

**8** On pages 14 and 15 it was explained that many of our cathedrals were once served by monks who lived in monasteries attached to their cathedrals. Although most of the monastery buildings were destroyed on the order of Henry the Eighth, traces of them can still be seen in many cathedrals. The best preserved parts are the cloisters where the monks once spent so much of their time, writing and reading. As can be seen in picture 12 below, the chapter house where the monks met with their prior, is usually found along the eastern side of the cloisters.

**9** In all cathedrals there are small enclosed areas with their own altars. These are chapels and the most important ones are the 'Lady chapels' dedicated to the Virgin Mary. When they were first built, Lady chapels were always very beautiful with stained glass and painted walls. Many of them were stripped of their decoration by Cromwell's men but traces of their original splendour can often be found. Colour can sometimes be seen inside deeply cut carvings which have since been whitewashed over.

**12** This is a plan of a typical cathedral showing the parts mentioned in these two pages:

**10** Although chantry chapels were destroyed at the time of Henry the Eighth, some have survived in cathedrals. Prayers are no longer said in them for the souls of the people who endowed them. Nowadays, prayers are said in cathedrals, not only for these people, but for everybody who has in some way helped the church.

**11** In the very early days of Christianity, the first Christians were hunted out by the Romans. Those killed for their faith were honoured by other Christians as martyrs or saints. Their bodies were buried in underground places called 'catacombs', outside the city. These catacombs became places of pilgrimage for later Christians and churches were often built over them. It became the custom for underground chapels to be built beneath all new cathedrals and many of these underground chapels can still be seen. They are called 'crypts'.

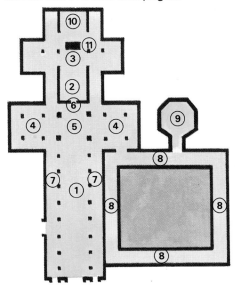

| | | |
|---|---|---|
| 1 Nave | 5 Crossing | 9 Chapter house |
| 2 Choir | 6 Pulpitum | 10 Lady chapel |
| 3 Sanctuary | 7 Aisles | 11 High Altar |
| 4 Transept | 8 Cloister | |

# Cathedrals to visit

## England

1. Canterbury
2. Rochester
3. London — St Paul's
4. London — Southwark
5. Guildford
6. Chichester
7. Portsmouth
8. Winchester
9. Salisbury
10. Wells
11. Bristol
12. Exeter
13. Truro
14. Gloucester
15. Oxford
16. St Albans
17. Chelmsford
18. Worcester
19. Hereford
20. Birmingham
21. Coventry
22. Lichfield
23. Leicester
24. Peterborough
25. Ely
26. Bury St Edmunds
27. Norwich
28. Derby
29. Southwell
30. Lincoln
31. Chester
32. Sheffield
33. Manchester
34. Liverpool
35. Blackburn
36. Bradford
37. Wakefield
38. York
39. Ripon
40. Durham
41. Newcastle
42. Carlisle

## Scotland

1. Glasgow
2. Edinburgh
3. Perth
4. Oban
5. Dundee
6. Aberdeen
7. Inverness
8. St Andrews
9. Brechin

## Wales

1. Llandaff
2. St Davids
3. Newport
4. St Asaph
5. Bangor

## N. Ireland

1. Belfast
2. Londonderry
3. Armagh
4. Newry
5. Downpatrick
6. Dromore
7. Monaghan
8. Clogher
9. Enniskillen

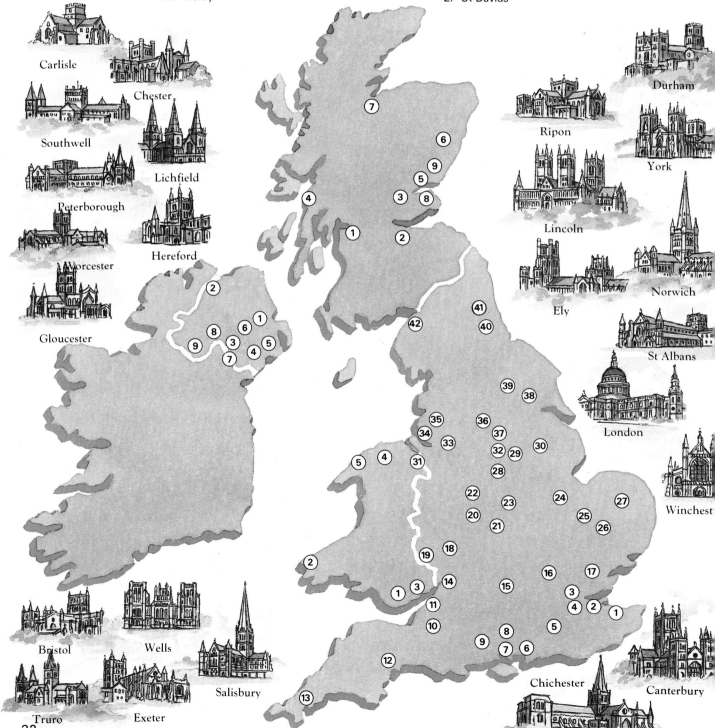

Carlisle
Chester
Southwell
Lichfield
Peterborough
Hereford
Worcester
Gloucester

Durham
Ripon
York
Lincoln
Norwich
Ely
St Albans
London
Winchest

Bristol
Wells
Salisbury
Truro
Exeter
Chichester
Canterbury